Mindfulness for Kids

A Guide to Raising Calm, Focused & Curious Children

Mitchell Wagner

Table of Contents

Introduction

First off, many thanks for the purchase of the book:

Mindfulness For Kids:
A guide to raising calm, focused & curious children

Just an editing note at the start: I have chosen pronouns "he" and "she" arbitrarily. There is no gender bias intended. The exercises and examples are all unisex.

By taking action and learning about mindfulness, you have taken a real, positive step toward achieving the most important goal as a parent; having your kid become a great adult.

You and I both know what that looks like. She is kind, helpful, hard working, can acquire and hold down a good job and copes well with the stresses you know she will be faced with.

Speaking of stresses, I think this generation of parents has it much harder.

Parents, usually both, work, so there is less supervision and nurturing. If you are a single parent, this is obviously more difficult.

Parents have so much more responsibilities (with work and children's activities) that are stressing us out. Gone are the days, it seems, when kids are encouraged to play outside all day.

Screens (cell phones, TV, computers) have replaced free range outdoor time. As a result, kids are getting heavier and their brains have become more prone to severe reactions when even the littlest of issues come their way.

There is massive psychological impact social media has on a kid's self-worth.

Processed food dominates the grocery shelves. Many of these products are laden with ingredients I can't even pronounce.

The world's wealth has shifted to a larger number of countries. Our kids will now have to compete globally for better jobs. The competition and stress will intensify.

Helping your child to develop good habits takes time, effort and sticking with your convictions. However, we have difficulty coping with all that life has in store. So, we tend to either let kids have what they want or we blow up quickly and /or disproportionately when they behave badly.

Mindfulness is not a magic bullet. However, if you can cultivate mindfulness habits in your family, it will, in the long run, better allow you and your children to manage their ups and downs.

Speaking of ups and downs, I love the explanation of mindfulness benefits provided by Mathieu Ricard, a Buddhist monk, originally from France who now resides in Nepal, and has been labeled by scientists as the "happiest man in the world". He suggests that without mindfulness, it is like you are swimming on the surface of the ocean during a storm and the waves are the stresses in your life battering you about, whereby a mindfulness practice allows you to thrive at the bottom of the ocean where the waves of stress have little or no impact - only calmness.

Researchers have revealed the three main benefits to a mindfulness practice. One, you are more able to focus on things that you want to focus on instead of letting your mind wander to past mistakes or future worries. Two, it allows you to better regulate against the harmful effects of negative emotions. Three, it frees you from the rigid personality characteristics defined by yourself or others. I'm always amazed that something so simple like paying attention to your breathing for 20 minutes/day could have such a profound impact!

So, it is important to start cultivating good, healthy, and constructive mindfulness habits at a tender age so they carry through a lifetime. These habits will help kids become mentally stronger, healthier, and more focused as they grow. Now, don't despair if your kids are older (teenagers) before you start a mindfulness practice. We know through research that a brain can form new neural pathways even in the elderly.

This book: Mindfulness for Children is a guide to teaching mindfulness techniques for you and your kids. The main objective is to teach you mindfulness exercises to raise well-developed children, capable and ready to tackle life and to succeed.

The book has 5 chapters. Chapter 1 describes how the brain works and how mindfulness changes the brain physically for the better. Chapter 2 tries to convince you to adopt mindfulness practices as part of the process. Chapter 3 offers some really cool exercises for kids of all ages. Chapter 4 makes recommendations for other healthy habits that will ensure the best outcome for your kid.

Chapter 1 - The Mindful Brain

I cringe at thinking that this book will have an overly technical component to how the brain works. Frankly, I just want to provide some context on how the brain changes with a mindfulness practice....not to put you to sleep!

My intention is to have you understand how mindfulness impacts your brain in two distinct ways.

First, it trains your brain into spending more time thinking about your present moment experience instead of stewing over past mistakes and worrying about future "what-ifs". This is a learned skill much like reading, writing or arithmetic.

Second, and more importantly, mindfulness practice changes your brain's physiology. Your brain actually, literally, physically changes. It's analogous to a bicep muscle as it changes size and shape with lifting weights. So a brain, too, will change with mindfulness practice.

So, we can strengthen our mind. This is so great!

We know that genetics plays a large role in how your brain works. You are an introvert, an extrovert, good with numbers, or good with music. You are generally happy; you are generally sad. Not happy with your IQ - blame your parents!

Having said that, if I go back to my bicep example, if I take two people with two physically different looking body shapes, and I provide them with good nutrition and demand 10 weeks of bicep curls, both people will see improved tone and strength. The brain is the same. With the proper practice, you will make it stronger, more focused and healthier no matter what genetics have been bestowed upon you.

Our brain has parts that are responsible for different functions. Functions that have served us well since cave man days. There are not many creatures on this planet that have done so well to grow their species...well, maybe cockroaches!

Interestingly, the evolution of the human and, more specifically, the human brain hasn't changed much since the cave man days. The problem is that our technical innovations over the last 100 years have been meteoric - yet the brain has not evolved at the same pace to cope with all the noise.

One part of our brain, the reptilian brain, as it's known to us as laymen, is responsible for basic function...breathing, sexual drive, fight or flight response to name a few. The cerebral cortex, the brain bits behind your forehead is responsible for higher thinking...language, solving problems, empathy and such.

The important thing to know is that there is the tug of war between higher thinking and "fight and flight" response. The other important point is that you can't access the higher thinking brain when the reptilian brain "fight or flight" response has been triggered.

The child you want is one that activates his cerebral cortex all the time. If you could de-active the "flight or fight" response, you and your children would have a much easier time coping with stress.

So what's the point of having a "fight or flight" response?

From an evolutionary point of view, "fight or flight" was the key to keeping our caveman ancestors alive when being attacked by a man-eating tiger. Adrenaline pours into the bloodstream preparing you for quick physical movements, your senses are heightened, and you react quickly and instinctually. The higher order thinking is put on hold until the threat has been eliminated. Yes, I speared the tiger or I managed to run to my campfire for protection. The "flight or fight" response saved his life. Have you ever tried getting close to a squirrel? With all the predators ready to pounce, you can understand why a squirrel's "flight" response is heightened and how that might be helpful for its survival.

So, I've mentioned that our brain has not evolved much or any since the invention of fire. The fact is, though, we are rarely in need, particularly in first world countries, to activate the "fight or flight" response. The most challenging aspect of this primitive response is that our brain will quickly and repeatedly active the "fight or flight" response for either real or perceived threats....sometimes, these perceived threats seem to loom continuously so we spend way too much time in this state.

Lucky is the boy or girl who seems to naturally roll through life, able to stay present without getting too worked up about things. Perhaps, these kids are the next evolutionary jump in human evolution. Unfortunately, most of us have kids that are distracted, agitated, depressed or stressed out.

Mindfulness practice is an important strategy to having your kid spend time in the cerebral cortex, the higher thinking part of the brain.

Here's the research. Scientists recruited a large number of people to participate in a mindfulness meditation study. They MRI scanned the brains of people at the beginning of the study to set a baseline. Half of the group participated in an 8 week (30 minutes/day) meditation practice; the other half did not. The researchers scanned both groups of people at the end of the meditation sessions. What they found was incredible: The parts of the brain associated with higher brain function increased in size and the reptilian brain actually shrunk. Also, those that meditated were reporting higher levels of happiness, focus and empathy than those that did not participate in the meditation classes.

So, how might this benefit your child?

Success in school

Mindfulness accelerates learning and memorizing power, thus enabling children to grasp challenging concepts easily. Moreover, the practice of mindfulness in children enhances cognitive and creative abilities as well as problem-solving skills, allowing children to perform better at various extracurricular activities.

Cultivates mental stability

Regular practice of mindfulness helps children become mentally grounded. Children go through many problems at home and school. This creates lots of mixed up feelings, emotions, and thoughts in their mind.

Instead of discussing their feelings with their parents or a trustworthy person, many children keep these emotions locked up inside. This does them more harm than good and often results in anxiety, stress, and depression. Letting negative thoughts and emotions stew without the skills to "let them go" casts an adverse effect on a child's mental and physical well-being, which can cause a child to lag behind his peers.

Helps them deal with ADHD

ADHD is the acronym for Attention Deficit Hyperactivity Disorder. Originally known as ADD (attention deficit disorder), ADHD is a condition characterized by signs such as hyperactivity, impulsivity, and inattentiveness. It normally affects young children and negatively influences their focus, concentration, and attention span.

Research shows that mindfulness is an effective technique to deal and eventually eliminate ADHD in kids. A research study printed in the Journal of Child and Family Studies in 2011 showed that an eight-week long mindfulness program helped children aged between eight and twelve manage ADHD successfully. Mindfulness helps reduce stress, increases attention span, and provides peace of mind in children making it easier for them to handle the disorder easily.

Leads to self-actualization

Self-actualization is the aspect of achieving and unlocking your full potential or more simply put, being the best 'you' you can be. All parents try their best to raise their children in a manner that helps them unleash their full potential and discover their hidden abilities and to make them well-rounded children.

Teaching your children mindfulness can help you accomplish this mammoth parenting goal. Research shows that mindfulness helps shape the personality and assists children in finding out, and achieving their full potential.

Helps dangerous health conditions

Mindfulness helps a child spend less time in the "fight or flight" response condition.

Hormones are released during the "fight or flight" response. These hormones are safe if released occasionally. However, if your kid is stressed all the time, the constant trickle of these hormones will lower his or her immune system. So, not only is he or she more susceptible to colds and flu, but there is evidence that suggests your kids are at risk to more serious health threats like cancer.

Chapter 2 - Walk the Talk

If you don't do what you say, your children won't trust you. If you try to teach them something you don't practice, even younger kids will be highly suspicious of your motives.

Secondly, like it or not, kids model your behavior and your actions; mine certainly do. I have this habit of throwing my gym bag in the front hallway of our home before getting settled. My wife has mentioned that she'd prefer I put it away. I think that's a good idea, but I never do it. Now, I've noticed that my two kids throw their school backpack in the front hallway and I'm forever tripping on them! Am I a hypocrite for demanding they hang up their stuff ? Do I have any credibility here? Will their behavior change? No way!

So, the first step to teaching children mindfulness is to become mindful yourself. This really is mandatory. Good News! This doesn't have to be difficult or time-consuming. And the Good, Good News is that it will lead to health benefits for you.

Include Mindful Meditation in your Morning or Evening Routine.

If you don't have a morning or evening routine, I highly recommend starting one. My morning routine has provided me and my followers with exponential happiness.

Here's my morning routine (as an example).

6:30 - wake up

6:31 - smile (even if I don't feel like it)

6:32 - spoon my wife (even if she doesn't feel like it)

6:34 - drink a glass of water

6:35 - meditate for 25 minutes

7:00 - 20 minutes cardio (I have my road bike mounted on a gizmo that allows me to ride indoors)

7:20 - weights and stretching

7:30 - COFFEE! Yes, my grand reward - it's usually a cappuccino

I do this every day, barring days I take my kid to hockey practice or when I'm ill.

Having a morning routine allows you to start your day strong and it will help bring out the best of you!

Mindful Meditation 101

Start with the basics

Sit in a comfortable chair or cushion and gently close your eyes. Keep your back straight, but comfortable. If you slouch, you will become drowsy and might nod off. Breathe normally without forcing your breath to be slow, fast, or deep. Think about the breath coming into the belly. Pay attention to the sensations of your belly expanding and contracting. Alternatively, you can focus on the breath in your lungs or as the breath passes through your nose. Choose what works best for you. NOTE: YOUR MIND WILL WANDER OFF. This is normal and it will always happen. In the beginning, or when you have a lot on your mind, your mind will spend more time wandering than focusing on your breath. Try not to be too hard on yourself. As soon as you notice that your mind has wandered, gently bring it back to thinking about your breath.

As an alternative, instead of focusing on your breath, choose to focus on things that you hear (and the silence between the sounds). Again, as you mind wanders, gently bring it back to this anchor - the sounds that abound.

Pay attention to the moments of your day

We want your kids to live in the moment; not to dwell on the past or worry about the future.

Same applies to your thoughts.

During the day, try to pay attention to routine activities (eating, showering, brushing your teeth, driving to work...the list is endless). With time, you will more often than not, start paying attention with curiosity to your present moment experience. You will start paying attention to your kids' world too. And, those little details are where the joy is hiding!

Honestly, paying attention to your thoughts, emotions and your senses will unlock the door to a contented life.

Just tune into yourself throughout the day by asking the questions:

1. What am I thinking about?

2. What emotions am I feeling?

3. What are my senses telling me?

That is all you can think about...ever.

Learn with Kids

Participate in mindfulness exercises with your kids. You will find that, almost by osmosis, you will adopt a more mindful existence.

Chapter 3 - Techniques to Develop the Mindful Kid

Let's face it, the idea of your kid sitting quietly and focusing on his breath for extended periods, just, is not going to happen. Zero fun. But, what if you could teach your child a variety of games that require him or her to focus their attention?

A bit of a sidebar here. My experience is that video or computer games are the crack- cocaine of youth entertainment. My kids love cards and a host of other great board games. But, frankly, they can't compete with computer games. So, I have had to wean my kids off gaming as much as possible. It's tough, but the research supports my very unpopular stance with my kids. The good news is that after a week of screen time prohibition, my kids stop asking for it and fill in the time with other, more creative and interactive activities.

You can do these games with one child or more.

Mindfulness Meditation - Kid Style

To teach your child 'how to mindfully focus' on his or her breath...

Sit in a Quiet Peaceful Room: To begin, choose a quiet, serene place that helps the two of you focus on your breathing movements easily. You could sit outdoors, but make sure to select an area that isn't noisy. This way, you'll be able to concentrate on your breath.

Give your child a cushion to sit on if sitting on the floor is difficult or uncomfortable for him or her. Ask your child to either cross his or her legs or keep them straight extending forward. Next, ask the child to focus on their breathing as you learned in the last chapter.

Focusing on their breathing can be a little difficult for children since they aren't used to focus on something for long. However, the helpful tricks below can assist your child to become mindful of their breathing and bodily movements with a lot of ease.

Tips To Help Your Child Become More Mindful

Set the mood. Unless you like to make things amazingly difficult, don't start a mindfulness meditation session with your child (at any age) when they feel distressed, super hyper, hungry, or sick. If you can, pick a spot during their normal down time when there is peak calmness.

Prime the pump. OK, to help settle a child before a mindfulness session, start with an activity that is calming. For example, before I sit down with my two little whirling dervishes to meditate for say 5 minutes, I'll have them read on their own, solve a sudoku puzzle, paint or draw for 20 minutes. I give them so much latitude on this; just as long as it does not involve any screen or it doesn't get their heart rate above 100 beats per minute.

Ask the child to practice with their breathing buddy: A breathing buddy is a toy, preferably a stuffed animal that your child can use while practicing mindfulness breathing. Props can pique your child's curiosity and make your sessions more enjoyable.

Ask the child to lie flat on their back on an exercise mat and place their breathing buddy on the top of their belly. Now, ask them to take deep breaths and focus on how their buddy moves upwards and downwards with the motion of their belly. This will certainly excite your child because most children enjoy new exercises and techniques.

Tell your child that he or she must focus on how their breath 'swings' their buddy and if they become distracted, they should think of their stuffed toy. Practice this for about seven to ten minutes, or even for longer if the child does not become bored. A daily ten-minute practice is sufficient to help your child become familiar with mindfulness.

Place Hands on Belly: When you ask your child to lie down as a means to practice mindfulness meditation, ask him or her to gently place his or her hands on their belly and notice how their belly rises and falls with each inhalation and exhalation. This will be a fun-filled activity for your child and will accompany lots of chuckles and giggles.

Don't rebuke the child if he or she finds it too amusing and cannot control the giggling and laughter. Instead, laugh with them and enjoy the moment. Once, their laughter subsides and they no longer find it hilarious, sweetly ask them to focus on their belly's movements and their breathing.

Inquire About Their Feelings: Once the meditation session is over, ask your child how he or she feels and what they experienced. Find out if he or she felt more connected with their body and could feel every tiny movement that occurred in their body while they were breathing. This small discussion will help your child better understand the goal he or she is trying to achieve. The next time you practice mindfulness breathing together, your child will know what he or she wants to accomplish and can do a better job.

You should also find out if your child experienced any discomfort or troubling emotions during the practice. Use this practice as a way to bond with your child and find out the thoughts going on in his or her mind so you can change them with the help of mindfulness.

In the next chapter, we'll look at how to cultivate attention in children by helping them develop, nurture, and exercise their "attention muscle". This is a fantastic expression. If you can imagine that paying attention requires a muscle to do it, then paying attention to the things you want to pay attention to gets stronger with exercise.

Training Your Child's "Attention Muscles"

Once you've familiarized your child to mindful breathing, you can expand these sessions by teaching him how to become mindful of their entire body.

Most children find it hard to focus on something for long. Often, when children discover something new and exciting, their attention on that thing or experience does not last long before the child loses interest. This is healthy and normal during the early childhood development and experts state that children aged between two and six can only focus on something for about 4 to 20 minutes.

How to Train your Child's Attention Muscle

Let us look at techniques you can apply to develop your child's attention muscle, and in the process, increase his or her attention span, concentration, and alertness.

To train your child's attention muscle, we first need to ignite the flame of curiosity. Children rarely enjoy the same activity or exercise if it becomes repetitive. Therefore, try something different from the 'breathing buddy' and 'hands on belly' techniques to enhance your child's attention span and focus.

Below are alternate mindfulness exercises guaranteed to spark curiosity in your little one.

Mindful Eating

Mindfulness in eating is an interesting activity that can train your child to become more attentive in an easy, fun way. When you sit together for a meal, tell your child that you are going to add a little excitement to the meal by changing it into a game.

Tell your child to take a few deep breaths and then ask him to eat their meal one bite at a time. Each bite of food is on its own journey from the plate to the fork to the mouth, down the throat and finally into the belly. Instruct the child to chew each bite very slowly and feel the texture, aroma, and flavor of the bite. When chewing a bite, the child must focus on the chewing action only and must not make another bite. If the child wants a drink, he must wait until the food has made its way to his stomach.

This simple practice will make your child curious about his or her food and will start asking you questions. Answer them, but make sure not to speak when the child is chewing or taking a bite.

Add a competitive twist to the game by tracking how many bites your child pays attention to. If they are old enough, provide them with a pencil and paper to track it themselves. If they get to 15 full attention bites, offer them a reward of your choosing. My kids are keen for anything with chocolate, so that's usually a good incentive for them. Focusing on each bite not only helps to build their attention muscle, it makes them slow down their eating to mark down their score (there are all sorts of digestive health benefits for slower, mindful eating). This exercise also calls attention to their personal integrity. Are they marking down a mindful bite when it's not a mindful bite? With humor and grace, these can be marvelous opportunities to set your bundles of joy down the right path.

Mindful Painting

Tell your child you need him to create a beautiful painting with his bare hands. Offer your child different color paints and ask him to dip his fingers into the colors and paint anything on the paper. Before the child paints, ask the child to take five mindful breaths and then start painting.

Have your child focus on how the paint feels on his fingers, to experience the feeling of running 'paint-dripping-wet hands' on a canvas or paper; coax him into experiencing the sense, touch and feel of the activity.

Ask the child to take another five breaths after ten minutes and continue with this practice for as long as they enjoy it. You can try the same exercise with building sandcastles, building structures with Legos, or any other activity that involves the use of hands. The idea is to help your child experience different textures and surfaces so they become mindful of their sense of touch and can use it to enhance their ability to focus on things.

Treasure Hunt

Plan a treasure hunt. Hide some toys in the backyard, garden, or a room in your house. If she is old enough, provide your daughter with a checklist of items to be ticked off when it has been found. If she's not old enough, start with a small number of her most memorable stuffed toys. Provide your daughter with a bag to collect the items. A reusable shopping bag works great.

Once the items have been collected, and you have congratulated your young Sherlock Holmes, have them sit down, close their eyes and reach into the bag and describe each item.

As your child grows and develops, he or she is bound to experience mixed feelings as he or she interacts with a new world, friends, environment, etc. In the next chapter of our mindfulness for children blueprint, we are going to outline how children and parents can use mindfulness as an effective tool to manage new and difficult feelings.

Coping with Difficult Emotions

Mindfulness helps you become calm, relaxed, and composed. The daily practice of being aware of your thoughts, emotions, and feelings has the natural by-product of paying attention to your own raw emotions instead of stewing in them and being subjected to their direct influence. It's almost like watching a person being angry, for example, instead of being angry yourself. You are not feeling the intensity of what he is feeling.

Imagine having the skill to take a fly on the wall perspective of your own self. It's hard to stay in the intensity of difficult emotions if you just plainly observe them.

By now, I'm likely preaching to the choir: teach your child how to use mindfulness to calm the mind when it's troubled.

No Bull Shit here. You'll have your work cut out for you. Kids, especially as they get older are not keen to share their feelings. However, the following mindful techniques will help your kid achieve more peace and build up trust with you in the process. You may find that it opens the lines of communication for healthy dialogue.

Focusing Inwards: Children Mindfulness Techniques for Handling Emotions, Feelings, and Internal Thoughts

Below are techniques you can use to teach your child how to be mindful of his or her feelings, emotions, and thoughts, and build his or her capacity to handle these emotions irrespective of their nature.

The Super Hero Mindfulness Game

Almost every child loves superheroes, be it Spiderman, Batman, Flash, Hulk, Wonder Woman, or Captain America. If she's younger, maybe that hero is Dora, the Explorer or Thomas, the Tank Engine. I'm sure you already know without asking. Your kid's lunch box or bed sheets are covered with its image. You can leverage her connection to this superhero to help your child become aware of his or her complicated feelings. Once there is awareness, she can better recognize these feelings, thoughts, and emotions and breathe them down.

Ask your child to play with you and bring his superhero figurine along. Tell your child you want to teach him or her a trick that will make them strong and powerful like their beloved superhero. Then, ask the child to take five or six deep breaths and imagine that they are the superhero.

If your son likes Batman, tell him to imagine that he is the real Batman. Now, ask him to close his eyes, focus on what it might be like at home, school or at sporting events as that superhero. Allow this fantasy to play out for a few minutes.

Now, ask him to think about being that same superhero again, only this time, ask your son to imagine having to overcome conflict or a difficult task. Let him think on this for a few more minutes then ask him to open his eyes. Ask him about his thoughts and if he discovered any intense feelings. If the answer is yes, take interest in his thoughts and feelings and ask more questions but don't sound pushy. Once you know the thoughts bothering him, tell him to look for its solution as his superhero does. He might come to his own conclusion to handle the situation with courage and confidence.

Practice the exercise at least once a week to understand the different thoughts and feelings your child is experiencing and guide him or her to resolve them effectively.

The Personal Weather Report Mindfulness Game

When you have a calm moment with your daughter, ask her to use the weather to describe how she is feeling (describe their mood). Give the child different weather options, such as windy, calm, rainy, tsunami, stormy, and sunny.

Ask your child to choose a weather condition that describes her mood, emotional state, or feelings at that very moment. This will prompt the child to think about his or her thoughts and emotions for a while and understand his or her current emotional state.

When the child gives you an answer, tell him or her that nobody can modify the weather outside, but everyone, including your child, can certainly change his or her inner weather. When a child learns this, it will help the child become more peaceful. If she chooses windy or stormy, gently, ask her why she feels that way.

She might become a little overwhelmed; if you need calm immediately, ask her to identify 5 red (color doesn't matter) objects in the area. Just that simple thoughtful task will help. Once she's a little calmer, ask her to focus on 5 breaths at her belly. Once the fear ebbs, continue exploring the reasons behind her mood. Don't force it. If it's too difficult for her to talk, give it time. After a handful of these moments, she will confide in you. She is beginning to understand that your intentions are not to criticize or to punish, but they are to help her navigate through rough waters.

Return to paying attention to the breath. Ask her to close her eyes and imagine having the power to place the bad weather in a big soap bubble and letting a gentle breeze blow it away. With each returning difficult feeling, ask her to imagine the bad feeling is a storm cloud in her stomach and she has the power to move it from her stomach to the inside of the soap bubble. Let her imagine it drifting away in the breeze. What's left in her stomach (where many of us hold tension) is the beautiful clear sunny sky.

Carry out these practices as many times as possible to help your child become aware of negative feelings and thoughts so he or she can learn how to manage them better.

Unburden the Young Mind

Mindfulness means to be open and curious about your present moment experience. It means to accept what you experience as it is without leaving the moment to fret about the past or worry about the future.

When you learn to live in the present, you are able to curb the storm of negative emotions erupting inside you. You observe the thoughts and emotions behind that storm and you will more effectively manage it.

This is exactly what you need to teach your kids so that they, too, can better regulate through difficult times.

For most children, childhood years are full of fun, play, excitement, enthusiasm, and love. But all children will suffer hardship; this is normal. And as difficult as this is for you, it is helpful for them to experience moderate hardship. In fact, these are critical life skills best learned at a young age.

In some cases, the hardship is not moderate. It is vile with long lasting implications. It may include bullying, verbal abuse, sexual harassment, neglect by a parent and more.

As much as we want to protect our kids with our mama bear instincts, we still need to teach our kids how to self-manage the negative emotions; that strife without coping skills can lead children down the wrong path.

Inner Peace: Mindfulness Techniques for Quelling the Inner Storms

The Past Doesn't Last

When your child is practicing a mindfulness meditation session with you, tell him that today you want to talk about the importance of letting go of past mistakes or troubles, and become more aware of the present.

Coax him into believing the past is just that, history, and it's the present moment that is most dear. If your child finds it difficult to understand, just ask him or her to breathe and think of the traumatic episode that has shattered him. Let him know he is safe right now and draw from him a small list of the blessings he has.

It's natural that he will return to his worry. Ask him to think about his favorite book or TV show. Tell him that the main character of this story wants to talk to him about his worries. Let him know that the character wants to write a book or make a TV show about his worry; during the new story, the main character destroys the worry and takes your son on the most fantastic journey EVER.

Instruct your child to imagine this character will stop whatever he's doing to help your child whenever he or she feels confused, disturbed, or annoyed.

Chapter 4 - Instill Compassion In Your Child

Kids who learn compassion will more likely pay attention to their present moment experience. Also, compassion is an attribute that can reduce the impact of his or her own suffering.

How to Instill Mindful Compassion in Your Child

I love the Cheryl Crow lyric: "It's not having what you want. It's wanting what you've got."

Wanting more and better things will never satisfy happiness cravings for long. And, you cannot learn to be compassionate to others unless you are content with what you have. When you are at peace with your life and are satisfied with whatever you are blessed with, you will express gratitude to others and have strong desires to help those less fortunate. Then you can entertain the notion of being happy.

Being at peace means you are able to look around and pay attention to those living with you and around you and seeing it as it is without the blinders on. It is suffering, clear and simple and your child is not desensitized, immune to it or embarrassed by it. With the proper encouragement from you, your children will want to provide those who are suffering with kindness and comfort. I probably won't get too much of an argument that we all desire our kids to live this way.

There are mindful exercises, to instill gracious and thankful behavior in your kids.

List of blessings

Before your kid goes to bed at night, ask him to give you a list of three things that they are grateful for. From my experience, you will hear or read some very endearing and creative items. If you are lucky to have your son or daughter journal at night, it will make for exceptional reading when he or she has kids of their own. Most importantly, it will help your child become aware of the blessings bestowed upon him or her, allowing him or her to express their gratitude fully.

Teach your child the value of helping others

Ask your kids to partake in helping out at your local soup kitchen. If there is no soup kitchen, volunteering at a food bank will do nicely. If your kids are like mine, you will hear anything from a groan to a flat out "no". You might have to be unyielding in this plan. Explain to your kids that you want to participate in helping others to feed your own soul. Do not even suggest it is to make them a better person. Using guilt or suggesting the benefits of this activity will negate the positive impact.

Before you arrive at the soup kitchen, explain to your kids that many people in your community are not as fortunate and need help from time to time. Tell your children that you want to help reduce suffering and are happy to lend a hand.

The impact of this time with your kids is amazing. The benefits are two-fold. First, helping someone in need is heart-warming and secondly, being part of a team that sets up, serves food, cleans dishes or whatever needs being done provides your child a stronger sense of purpose and humility.

Your family bond will strengthen. Your kids will trust you more.

Loving-Kindness Guided Meditation

Guided meditations are when someone leads you during a meditation session to "guide" your mind by their gentle instructions.

They are popular, in part, because it is easier to be mindful when you are being instructed along the way. There is less chance of your mind wandering and getting frustrated or bored with the process.

Of all guided meditations, "loving-kindness" meditations are the most popular. Consider a YouTube search and you will find one for you and your children.

They can be 5 minutes or much longer. But the theme is fairly consistent. You will be asked to direct loving-kindness thoughts toward others and accept the loving kindness directed back to you.

My suggestion is to get into the habit of using this technique as a tuck-in at bedtime.

Sending Loving-kindness . . .

I ask them to close their eyes get comfortable. I will hand them a gentle stone to keep them focused on an object. Then I say the following:

Send loving-kindness to yourself

Really love yourself.

Want yourself to be happy.

Think:

I love myself.

May I be free from anger.

May I be free from sadness.

May I be free from pain.

May I be free from difficulties.

May I be free from all suffering.

May I be healthy.

May my body be healthy and strong.

May I be filled with love for others.

May I be happy in my heart

May I be at peace in my heart.

I spread this loving-kindness out: first to my Mom and Dad

May Dad and Mom be free from difficulties.

May they be free from pain and sadness.

May they be free from wanting to collect things

May they be free from all suffering.

May Mom and Dad be healthy and happy.

May they have peace in their hearts

I send loving-kindness to both my brothers and sisters.

May they be free from sadness and anger.

May they be free from all suffering.

May they be happy and free.

May they be free from worrying

May they be well and happy.

May they have peace in their hearts

I send loving-kindness to my teachers and the kids at school.

May they be free from sorrow and suffering.

May they be free from anger and difficulties.

May they be happy.

Free from all difficulties and sadness.

May they be well and happy.

May they have peace in their hearts

I send love now to all the people and all animals and all plants everywhere on this earth.

May all beings on the planet be free from suffering.

May they be free from sadness.

May they be happy, truly happy.

May they be at peace.

I open my heart and accept love and kindness from every being and creature in return.

I let that love into my heart.

May there be peace.

Following the meditation, each child receives a hug/kiss and an "I love you." I lie there for a short time, then leave.

Chapter 5 - Increase Your Chances of Success

This chapter serves only one purpose. It's to suggest that a healthy life is not strictly about meditation and mindfulness. It's like jogging to get more fit, but having a cigarette when you finish. Bad example, but I think you get the point.

So, here is a bullet point list of my do's and don'ts to reap the benefit of yours and your kid's mindfulness practice.

Do's:

- Eat as much unprocessed food as you can afford. Normally, you find all this good stuff on the outside isles of your grocery store.

- Make sure your kid gets ample sleep. In most cases, 8 or 9 hours isn't enough.

- Let your kids fight, argue, and generally get into trouble. But...always make them accountable for their actions and don't let them get away with shit!

- Model your behavior. Act like the adults you want them to be.

- Play games with your kids (especially games outdoors). Families that play together, stay together.

Don'ts:

- Reduce or eliminate screen time. It's a brain killer - the research shows that your kids brain physically changes for the worse the more time they spend watching a screen (any screen).

- Don't let your kids be lazy. Chores, homework, sports, part time jobs, volunteering. My wife is a high school teacher. Without a doubt, kids from farms where they have a lot of chores make the best students. Hard work and a can-do attitude are the best attributes for scholastic success.

- Don't accept poor manners. A child won't go far in life if they can't treat people nicely and respectfully.

- Don't be friends with your kids (at least until they've reached their twenties). Your kids need to know that your relationship is parent/child and the boundaries this implies. It certainly doesn't mean you can't be friendly and spend time together having fun, but your kid always needs to be reminded that how they treat their friends is not how they treat you.

This isn't the most comprehensive list of do's and don'ts, nor do I offer evidence that these principles are well-founded. However, from my experience and those that I work with, if you adopt some or all of these ideas, if you haven't already, you will find that your mindfulness sessions with your kids will be more meaningful and effective.

Conclusion

It is your job as a parent to teach your child techniques and skills to help him or her to become a balanced and kind person who has full control of his or her emotions, and who can channel their inner power easily.

Mindfulness meditation and other mindful practices are techniques that you can apply to help kids become better prepared to meet today's (and tomorrow's) challenges.

Even if it seems overwhelming to take on another "thing" in you busy day, if you can make room for 5 minutes/day as part of a morning or bedtime routine, you will make physical changes in your brain and your child's brain, improving mental health.

New ways of doing things are easier if you build them into a daily routine. Please consider this idea and may you and your children have peace.

Thank you and good luck!

Made in the USA
San Bernardino, CA
25 October 2018